# Shy Spaghetti and Excited Eggs

Published by
Magination Press
An Educational Publishing Foundation Book
American Psychological Association
750 First Street, NE
Washington, DC  20002

For more information about our books, including a complete catalog,
please write to us, call 1-800-374-2721, or visit our website at www.maginationpress.com.

Book design by Sandra Kimbell

Printed by Worzalla, Stevens Point, WI

Library of Congress Cataloging-in-Publication Data

Nemiroff, Marc A.
Shy spaghetti and excited eggs : a kid's menu of feelings / by Marc Nemiroff
and Jane Annunziata; illustrated by Christine Battuz.
p. cm.
ISBN 978-1-4338-0956-9 (hbk.) -- ISBN 978-1-4338-0957-6 (pbk.)  1. Emotions in children--Juvenile literature. 2.
Emotions--Juvenile literature.  I. Annunziata, Jane. II. Battuz, Christine. III. Title.

BF723.E6N35 2011
155.4'124--dc22
2010048836

Manufactured in the United States of America
10  9  8  7  6  5  4  3  2  1

# Shy Spaghetti
# and Excited Eggs
## A Kid's Menu of Feelings

by Marc Nemiroff, PhD
and Jane Annunziata, PsyD

illustrated by Christine Battuz

Magination Press • Washington, DC
American Psychological Association

Welcome to the Feelings Restaurant.

There are lots of different kinds of feelings.

Here's the menu!

# *Feelings Restaurant*

Worried
Watermelon

Happy Hot Dog

Shy Spaghetti

Sad Spinach

Surprised
Strawberries

Sorry
Steak

Angry Apples

Excited Eggs

Scared Shrimp

Lonely Lettuce

Confused Cupcakes

All feelings are OK!
No feeling is *right* or *wrong!*

**100% discount** *when you show your feelings in a good way!*

When you feel **happy**, you feel like everything is wonderful! Maybe something good or special has happened. Or, you could just be having a very good day.

Usually we feel happy in our whole bodies and we smile or laugh a lot.

But sometimes the happy feelings get too big and you start to get really silly and bother other people. Then you need to get back in charge of your happiness.

This is easy.

First, you need to know that you are too silly. (Usually a mom or dad will tell you.) You might be talking very fast and loud or you might not be able to stop laughing.

You will need to slow down. Here's how. Count all your fingers and breathe in and out slowly until you feel regular happy again.

**Worries** are thoughts or feelings that bother you.

They make you nervous.

Worries start when kids think a lot about things that might go wrong or that already happened that didn't feel right.

Sometimes you can be so full of worries that you can't relax or sleep well.

The more you worry, the bigger your worries get!

What Can You Do?

1. Close your eyes.

2. Take a deep breath using only your nose. Do this slowly.

3. When your tummy is full of air, get ready to breathe out.

4. Pretend you are going to blow up a balloon.

5. Slowly breathe all the air into the pretend balloon. Think about blowing your worries into the balloon. Do this five times.

6. Imagine the balloon is floating away and taking your worries with it.

The spaghetti is too shy to come out!

**Shy** is when you are nervous being around other people, especially other kids. Shy is a little bit like hiding from other people. You worry about letting other people know you. You might not even want people to look at you.

Shy is when you worry too much that you'll say or do something that other kids won't like or will laugh at. You might worry that people won't like you.

Here are some things
WE do when we feel shy:

We take deep
breaths in and
out really slowly
five times.

I practice talking
and sharing my ideas at
home. I make-believe that
my mom and dad are
other kids and I say and
do things to pretend
I'm not shy.

Become the boss
of your shyness!
Tell yourself:
"I can do this."

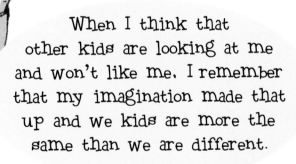

When I think that
other kids are looking at me
and won't like me, I remember
that my imagination made that
up and we kids are more the
same than we are different.

Everyone gets scared sometimes.
Other words for *scared* are afraid, frightened, or fearful.

Sometimes there are things that are really, truly scary, that ANYBODY would be afraid of.

But sometimes, your imagination turns safe things into scary things. This usually happens when you are upset.

A grown-up like your mom or dad can usually
help you figure out why you are upset.

Next time you're scared, remember how good it feels to be brave.

If you're not scared first, you never get the chance to be brave.

**Sad** is when you don't feel happy inside. Sad is when you can't think of things to make you smile. When you're sad, it's hard to have fun and you don't have a lot of energy. That's because you can feel sad in your whole body.

If you keep any feeling that bothers you deep inside (like a secret), you might start to feel worse. This happens with sad feelings a lot. Here's what you can do to move the feelings from inside you to outside you.

You can tell someone how you feel.

You can draw your sad feelings.

You can use your toys to play your sad feelings.

You can do some exercise that moves your whole body.

You can think about things that make you happy and make pictures of them in your mind.

The chef has a problem. He burned the steak!

He is full of regret. That means he feels so **sorry** and he wishes he hadn't done it. He is **embarrassed** because he made a mistake. He doesn't want to disappoint anybody.

## What Can You Do?

He can make a new steak. That's like fixing his own mistake. (Get it: Mis-steak?)

He can talk to himself and tell himself that everybody makes mistakes sometimes.

He can apologize and say, "I'm sorry." Or he can do something extra.

You might not want to say *I'm sorry* because you may be embarrassed. You might even think that saying *I'm sorry* is like saying *I'm wrong* or *I'm bad*. Saying *I'm sorry* is a brave thing to do. And you will almost always feel better when you apologize. The other person will too.

**Excited** is when you're having a really good time or you're really looking forward to something and you just can't wait.

Being excited is fun!

But when you feel too excited, that ISN'T so fun. When you're too excited, you're not the boss of your feelings anymore and that never feels good!

You might talk too loud, or talk too much.
You might even say the same thing over and over.

And you might have trouble sitting still or keeping your hands to yourself.

Look at yourself and ask: Am I the boss of my feelings, or are my feelings the boss of me? If you are not in charge of your feelings, here's what you can do.

Stop what you are doing!

Get calm.

1. Count your fingers and toes to yourself.
2. Leave the room for a while.
3. Get a drink of water.
4. Find a quiet place, close your eyes, and breathe in and out slowly.

If you need help doing these things, ask a grown-up in charge for help.

You will feel so good being the boss of your feelings again.

The lettuce is **lonely.**

Lonely can be when you really ARE alone, like when there's no one to play with. And lonely is also when you are feeling left out even when lots of other kids are around.

Feeling left out is when you don't know what to say or how to act around other kids. You feel like you don't belong.

Sometimes lonely can be boring and sometimes lonely can be sad. Lonely is a hard feeling.

One way to help a lonely feeling is to keep yourself busy and play on your own. But make sure you don't miss out on doing something fun that you want to do with other kids!

Be brave! Remember how good it feels when you do go over and start playing or talking?

You can also look for someone to play with or talk to.

The lettuce is going to do it and SO CAN YOU.

Lots of different feelings go with **Angry**.

Sometimes angry can start with small feelings.

**Annoyed** is being mini-mad. **Grumpy** is like a long bad mood.
**Irritable** is when every little thing bothers you. **Frustrated** is not having patience with yourself or with other people. Frustrated is when you want something and you can't have it. This can be SO disappointing!

These small feelings can get bigger, until you are REALLY angry!

You might feel SO angry that you think you could explode.

One thing you might do is have a great big temper tantrum.
A temper tantrum is when your whole body gets angry.

You're SO stupid!

When you are this **angry**, it's hard to think clearly.

Sometimes kids use action and words in mean ways to show how angry they are.

Other times kids show their **angry** feelings by doing the opposite of what they are supposed to do.

There are also quiet, small ways to show that you are mad or that something is really bothering you.

These are ways to show your angry feelings without even saying a word.

Sometimes it's hard to show angry feelings at all.
They get stuck inside you, like apples in a pie.

This is good for the pie, but NOT a good feeling for kids.

(We don't want you OR the pie to explode!)

And if no one knows
that you are mad,
they can't help you
feel better.

What to do when you are mad
(or when you are mini-mad and want to avoid getting mega-mad):

1. KNOW IT BEFORE YOU SHOW IT. Know what is making you angry before you do anything. A grown-up can help you.

2. Draw a picture of your mad feelings.

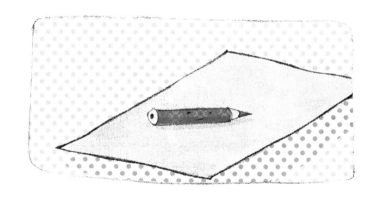

3. Play out your angry feelings with your toys.

4. Use your body in good ways to get your angry feelings out.

Exercise is a great way to feel better when you are mad. You can

or

or

or walk as fast as you can. The good thing about walking is that you can do it anywhere.

5. You can also use your body to help yourself feel calm:
Breathe in and out slowly.
Count to 1-2-3-4-5-6-7-8-9-10 slowly.
Close your eyes and make a picture in your mind of something that helps you relax.

And, most importantly, USE YOUR WORDS!

Practice saying "I'm mad at you because…" or "I'm so annoyed right now."

If you use words like these, then you don't have to worry that you will hurt someone's feelings or they will get mad at you. And you will feel proud of yourself, too!

Feeling angry is like having any other feeling. What matters is how you show it!

A **surprise** is when something happens that you weren't expecting.

Most surprises are good ones. Those are the ones everybody likes because they are fun and make you feel good. Surprises make everyone have big feelings all at once.

Some surprises are not good ones. That's when something unexpected happens that doesn't make you feel good. Kids REALLY don't like it when that happens.

You might feel **disappointed** (like if your friend can't come over to play), **bothered** (like if your brother or sister changes the television channel when you're not looking), or **shocked** (like if a loud noise happens while you're doing something quiet).

Kids really don't like bad surprises!

The biggest thing to remember when a bad surprise happens is:

DON'T LET YOUR FEELINGS TAKE OVER.

Stay in charge of them. Always be the boss of your own feelings. Don't forget:

Bad surprises don't happen very much.
They usually don't last long.
They usually aren't serious (like loud noises).

What also helps is to think about what made the bad surprise happen. Figuring it out helps the feelings not bother you so much anymore.

The cupcakes are **confused**!

They don't know what flavor they are.

Being confused means that you
- Feel all mixed up
- Can't figure something out
- Have jumbled-up thoughts or feelings inside you
- Don't understand what's happening
- Are puzzled

Kids don't like to feel confused!

When you DO feel confused, the most important thing to do is to GET THE FACTS.

Ask questions. Get answers. You can ask a friend sometimes...

...but grown-ups know the most facts of all.

WHEN YOU KNOW, YOU FEEL BETTER.

You can also be **confused** when you have two different feelings at the same time that don't go together.

Maybe one day you feel **angry** at mom or dad. This is confusing and uncomfortable because you love your parents so much.

Remember that loving feelings are always bigger and stronger than angry feelings. And if you just give your feelings a little time, the loving feelings will push the angry feelings away.

All mixed feelings usually work this way. If you just w…a…i…t, one feeling becomes stronger and the other feeling becomes smaller and goes away.

Mixed feelings are normal. Everybody has them!

Actually,
ALL feelings are normal...

We're ALL full of feelings.

...but they're not always easy.
That's why kids need help figuring them out.

AND NOW YOU KNOW HOW!

# Note to Parents

Kids often find it hard to express their feelings in constructive ways, enjoy their "good feelings," and cope with their unpleasant emotions. Learning about feelings is an important first step to doing the difficult work of coping with life's challenges, and expressing and experiencing life's joys. This book explores an array of the basic feelings that younger children experience, both the easier feelings such as excitement and the harder feelings such as anger.

### Label Feelings

Children often learn what they are feeling from their parents. One of the most important things you can do to teach your children about feelings is to label them—that is, to give them a name. This sounds very basic, but it is the foundation upon which all understanding of feelings is built. Children experience their feelings, and know that they are indeed feelings, but they don't always know what to call them.

## Be a Role Model

Another way you teach your children about feelings is by being a role model. They will observe you labeling your own feelings, expressing your feelings in appropriate ways, and staying in control even when you are stressed. You also comment on what other people are feeling. In other words, the world of feelings becomes part of the fabric of your conversations with your children. This is a lot like how you talk to and teach your children about letters or numbers or animals whenever the opportunity arises.

## Read Books and Talk

You can use *Shy Spaghetti and Excited Eggs* in several ways. Although it is not likely to be a book that one reads straight through in a single sitting, some children will enjoy listening to you read it, or reading it themselves, over several nights. Young and even not-so-young kids enjoy sharing a book with a parent, and reading together is often a wonderful springboard for discussion between children and parents.

## Learn to Manage

Children may not understand the nuances involved in emotions, and often have particular difficulty knowing how to manage their own feelings. Even a benign feeling such as happiness needs to be managed if it becomes "too big." *Shy Spaghetti and Excited Eggs* is primarily intended as a playful reference for children and their parents, a book to be enjoyed in segments and something to refer to when your children are experiencing or having difficulty with their feelings. Each feeling in *Shy Spaghetti and Excited Eggs* has suggestions for managing it when it becomes "too much," or too uncomfortable, or if a child presents problems in behavior because of her feelings.

You are the best resource for helping your child find ways to understand and manage emotions. However, if you find that your child becomes distressed or feelings interfere with daily activities, we recommend consulting a child psychologist for further guidance.